Chicken Bristles:
A CHILDHOOD REMEMBERED

Chicken Bristles:
A CHILDHOOD REMEMBERED

Teach your children to choose the right path, and
when they are older, they will remain upon it.
--Proverbs 22:6 (NLT)

E J Lewis

XULON PRESS

Xulon Press
2301 Lucien Way #415
Maitland, FL 32751
407.339.4217
www.xulonpress.com

© 2021 by E J Lewis

All rights reserved solely by the author. The author guarantees all contents are original and do not infringe upon the legal rights of any other person or work. No part of this book may be reproduced in any form without the permission of the author. The views expressed in this book are not necessarily those of the publisher.

Due to the changing nature of the Internet, if there are any web addresses, links, or URLs included in this manuscript, these may have been altered and may no longer be accessible. The views and opinions shared in this book belong solely to the author and do not necessarily reflect those of the publisher. The publisher therefore disclaims responsibility for the views or opinions expressed within the work.

Unless otherwise indicated, Scripture quotations taken from the Holy Bible, New Living Translation (NLT). Copyright ©1996, 2004, 2007 by Tyndale House Foundation. Used by permission of Tyndale House Publishers, Inc.

Printed in the United States of America

Paperback ISBN-13: 978-1-66283-293-2
Ebook ISBN-13: 978-1-66283-294-9

Table of Contents

Preface vii

The Windmill 1

The Family 5

School Days 12

Chicken Bristles 22

Lost 26

Wild (?) Animals 30

Flood 38

Pickup Adventures 41

Bullies 47

Music 51

New Dress 54

Chicken Bristles

OUTHOUSE AND CISTERN	57
VACATION	61
TUMBLEWEED CHRISTMAS	65
CHURCH	68
GARDENING AND GOOD EATING	71
BABYSITTING	76
4-H	82
COUNTY FAIR	92
THIS AND THAT	99
ABOUT THE AUTHOR	106

Preface

My brothers introduced me to a book titled, "Rivers of Wind", by Gary Penley. Gary attended the same high school we did and graduated with my brother, Roger's, class. Gary wrote about his growing up on a hardscrabble farm south of Lamar, Colorado. We grew up on a farm north of Lamar. We grew up thinking we had a rough life, but after reading Gary's book, I thought we had it fairly easy. It was a lot of hard work, but we had a lot of fun times, too. After reading his book, I started thinking about many of the things I had done and how they had influenced my life. We had many good times, bad times and hard times. Through it all, we had fun and laughter and knew we were loved. I treasure all my memories and am thankful for the person I am today. Thanks, Gary, for giving me the boost I needed to bring those memories to life again and put them on paper for others to know and share. Maybe others will

be moved by this book to share their stories for posterity, even if it is only with family and friends.

The Windmill

Windmills! Something not seen much anymore. Those still existing in America are usually standing unused in a farm or ranch field somewhere or maybe they are the small, decorative types standing in yards as simply decoration. In my growing up years these large structures, usually anywhere from twenty to forty feet or more high, were widely used on the arid plains to bring water to the surface, pumping it into large tanks used for watering livestock. They were also free sources of entertainment for children living on farms with few options available for pleasure.

As a child, I grew up on several different farms in southeastern Colorado. Some of them had a windmill fairly close to the house we lived in and had a big tank for watering the livestock. On hot summer days that tank also served as a form of swimming pool for us hot, dirty children. It definitely wasn't the most sanitary place but it was wet and cool. We certainly enjoyed it, sanitary or not. The windmill also served as a tower for daring adventurers, which my two older brothers excelled at. Of course, I, as the younger, tag-a-long sister, had to follow and do everything my older brothers did. Sometimes this got me into trouble.

One of my earliest memories involved one of those windmills. Kenny was four years older than me and Roger was two years older. This particular adventure occurred when I was probably only three or four so we were all still young. The boys liked to climb (as boys do) on the windmill's structure, so I had to do as they did and climb too. We had probably been warned many times about not climbing around on it because of how dangerous it could be. But, hey, we were children and didn't always heed instructions very well. We didn't have cell phones, or any type of phone, video games, TV or even many toys. We had to create our own fun and the windmill and tank were a big part of that.

I can't remember the exact circumstances of why or how, I just remember being on the top of that windmill, running around on the platform housing the inner workings of the pumping mechanism. I was just running around up there, laughing and having a wonderful time. It must have been exhilarating to be that high in the air, able to see everything for a long distance. It was probably only by the grace of God and His protection that I wasn't swept off by the rotating blades that turned with the wind to run the pumps. Maybe it was a calm day and the blades weren't turning. Of course,

The Windmill

my mother didn't think it was nearly as much fun as I did. I can't even remember anything else about the situation, not even how I got up or down. Recounting the incident many years later with my younger brother, he seemed to remember being told that my mother had to climb up there somehow and get me down. He also told me she had been afraid of heights. I guess mothers become fearless when it comes to protecting their children. Or maybe they just swallow their fear and do what has to be done in the situation. I don't remember what my punishment, if any, was. I never climbed it again though. That memory is only about the joy and laughter I experienced. In my mind, I can still see myself enjoying the moment.

A windmill on the plains. The one I climbed may not have been quite this tall.

Chicken Bristles

I think that windmill was the cause of another memory, not mine this time, but I remember the telling of it. My brother, Kenny, came running into the house and told Mama, "I need the pliers. Roger's arm is crooked and I need to straighten it out." It seems Roger had fallen, probably while climbing the windmill tower, and broken his arm. We had no telephone and Mama didn't drive, so I'm not sure how we got him to the doctor. Maybe there was a neighbor close enough to send for or maybe Daddy was working in the field close enough to the house that we could send for him. Somehow the arm got set, he healed, and I don't think he has had any more problems with it. Sometimes I wonder how we ever survived childhood. But we did and it's amazing to look back and remember all the fun times we had. Most children today will never have the options we had or the dangers we survived to grow into adulthood.

The Family

The family unit began in Nebraska. Daddy was born and raised in Missouri and Mama in Nebraska, where they met. Daddy as a single man had gone there to work on a farm. Mama was also working at the same farm as household help. They established their home there after they married. Maureen was the oldest child. Kenny came two years later and Roger two years after that. I was fourth in line and came along two years later, born in June 1944. Mama always told me that Maureen was tired of brothers and said that if I was another boy, she was sending me back. Lucky for me I was a girl.

The young family before leaving Nebraska: September 1944

The Family

Our family ancestry is a mixed bag of German, English and Scottish, with a few other minor nationalities thrown in for good measure. We were always told by Daddy that one of our grandmothers (not sure how many greats) was American Indian and that she was a Tennessee Indian. We had never heard of that tribe but just accepted it as truth. After all, our daddy had told it to us. I was always so proud of that Indian heritage. My older sister, Maureen, somehow determined that we were of Cherokee descent but we could never prove it. My daughter has done a lot of research into our genealogy and has not found any information that could substantiate that claim with any certainty.

Times were hard and work was hard to come by in the war years. Daddy had brothers living in Colorado by then and they told him they thought he could get farm work there. We migrated to Colorado sometime in the next year or so after I was born. The rest of my childhood years were spent in Colorado. Little wonder that I consider it my home state. Nebraska was simply my birthplace.

We lived on various farmsteads around Lamar, which is in the southeastern corner of the state. The land there is very arid and much of it is strictly dryland farming. There is also a lot of irrigated land due to its close proximity to the Arkansas river, which carries runoff water from snow melt in the mountains. A system of irrigation canals was established in order to direct this water to various districts and their farms. Irrigation back then was not undertaken by those big rolling sprinklers that are seen in fields today. Water was moved via ditches created along the edge of each field. Canvas dams were manually placed in the ditch to stop the water. Cutouts were then made in the bank, allowing the water to rush out and flood the field. When that section of the field was sufficiently flooded from one side to the other, the dam was moved to another location and the process repeated until the entire field had been irrigated to satisfaction. The water had to be shared with all districts so it was only available at certain times. When it was your turn for water, you had to irrigate. Irrigation time plays a part in another of my memories which will be shared in another chapter.

More children were born into the family after we moved to Colorado. Ruby is four years younger than me and Roy came along two years later. Mama had told Kenny and Roger that if this baby was a boy, they could name him. Roy Rogers and Gene Autry were very popular and were my brothers' heroes, so they named him Roy Gene. Sherry was the last child and was born three years after Roy. With her birth, I ended up in the exact middle, three on either side. I was partially raised by the older ones and also had to help in the raising of the younger ones. That was just the way it was done in large families.

The Family

Our last family photo: December 1977

Where we lived depended on which farmer Daddy was working for at the time. The houses where we lived are remembered by the school districts in which they were located. The first place I can remember living was Channing. The three older children all started school there. I think we were living there when we got flooded. (That story in another chapter.) We then moved to the Hopewell district and then on to Carlton, where I started school. We moved to May Valley when I was in the second grade. All the rest of the children went to school there through the eighth grade. After that we had to go to the big town of Lamar for high school. All of these elementary schools were two rooms, four grades in each room, with one teacher per room. It was a great educational experience. We probably got as good as, or better, education than a lot of children get today.

I do remember the first house we lived in when we moved to May Valley. It was a small adobe house set on a small hill just across a field from the school house.

Our first house in May Valley. It was in much better shape then but still just as small.

That was the closest we ever lived to school. We didn't live there very long, but I have some memories from that house. I don't remember how it happened, but the older boys and the dog got sprayed by a skunk. What a time

The Family

Mama had getting rid of that smell. We were living in that adobe house when I got the mumps. We had been up the hill to a neighbor boy's birthday party. Later I complained to Mama that I must have helped blow up too many balloons because my jaws were sore. Turns out that wasn't the problem at all. I don't remember if any of the others kids got mumps at the same time, but we all seemed to share our childhood diseases. I don't remember where we were living when I got the measles but I must have been fairly young because I don't remember much about them, just that I did have them. I think I do remember that we had to be kept in a darkened room so that they wouldn't affect our eyes. I don't remember how long we lived in that house before the big house we lived in later was ready or why we had to wait to move into it. We lived in that big house until all of us were grown and moved away from home. Daddy retired from that farm job and he and Mama moved to town. The last time we were in Colorado and drove by to check on our old home, there was nothing there. The trees had been uprooted, burned or hauled away, the house torn down, and the cistern had been collapsed and filled in. The entire corner where we had lived had been leveled and turned into field. Only the memories have survived.

School Days

I started the first grade at Carlton. There was no kindergarten back then in rural schools, but maybe there was in the cities. We lived at least two or three miles from the school house and there were no school buses to take us. Mama didn't drive and Daddy went to work early. We had to walk. It wasn't so bad when the weather was nice, but not so good when it was rainy, cold and/or snowing. We kept each other company as there were four of us going at the same time. The first leg of the journey was along the main highway so we had to be careful of the traffic. Thank goodness it wasn't as heavily traveled back then as it is now. The next leg was down a gravel county road and lastly, a lane that led back through a field to where the school house stood. All in all, not a bad walk most of the time.

I don't remember much about that school year itself, but some of the happenings are etched in my memory. I

School Days

especially remember one of my classmates named Jimmy Mizeman. My brothers teased me unmercifully about him. I chased him around the playground a lot. (I think it was because I really didn't like him.) My brothers were always trying to get me to kiss him, but that wasn't my intention at all.

One incident I remember from that year was the only time I can remember getting into trouble at school. Daddy had always told us that if we got a spanking at school, we would get another one when we got home. (They still gave spankings back then.) I don't remember if it was Jimmy or another boy that sat behind me. Whoever it was, he was poking at me and it was irritating. I kept telling him to leave me alone. When that didn't do any good, I turned around and jabbed at his hand with my pencil. Naturally, the teacher didn't see him doing anything to me. She did look up just in time to see me jab at him. I was reprimanded and called to the front of the room which was embarrassing enough. She explained to me that what I had done was unacceptable behavior for a young lady. I would have to endure a spanking in front of everyone. She was a somewhat hefty lady, so when she sat down to have me bend over her lap for my spanking, there wasn't much lap. Before she could administer much of a swat, I slid right off her lap onto the floor. That made it funny for the whole room. I think it embarrassed her more than it did me and the dreaded spanking did not take place. I just got a good lecture about my behavior. I didn't get a spanking when I got home either. My folks must have thought it funny also and I wasn't to blame for the incident.

Another memorable time occurred while at that school. One day I got a terrible itch just behind my knee, right at the bend of it. Of course, I spent the entire day scratching at it. I was miserable. When I got home, I naturally showed it to Mama. She immediately diagnosed me as having chickenpox. By the next day I was broken out all over with the sores, so it was no school for me. I don't remember how long I had to stay home, but as I was getting over them, all of the older ones came down with the dreaded disease. Since they all had them at the same time, I had to walk to school by myself for a time. I don't remember exactly how long I had to walk alone, but it was terrifying for a first grader. I do remember one morning when I was walking along that highway by myself, Mr. Mizeman , one of our neighbors, came along on his tractor and offered me a lift. We had probably been cautioned many times about accepting rides from strangers, but he was a neighbor so I figured it would be okay for me to accept his offer. He let me stand behind him and hold onto the back of the tractor seat. It was a lot of fun and much better and faster than walking along that busy highway by myself.

Even with the four of us together, it sometimes seemed like a long walk. One hot afternoon, a stranger in a car stopped and offered us a ride. I think we discussed it and decided it would be okay since there were four of us and only one of him. We climbed in and explained where we lived, on the curve of the road. When we came to our driveway, he just kept driving, right on past the turn in. We were ready to go to battle to get him to stop. He might have gotten a few blows to the head and shoulders before he stopped the car. I think by then he was just as or more scared than we were. He explained that he thought we meant the next house on the next curve. We didn't ask him to turn around and drive us home. We were closer than we were when he gave us the ride, so we just finished the journey by walking. He immediately drove away on down the highway. We were very careful about accepting rides after that. Come to think of it, he might have been more cautious about offering rides to strangers.

Another memory of the early school days did not involve me, but I remember my mother telling of it many times. I think it must have been one of those times that were so memorable, it just couldn't be forgotten and had to be told over and over. It may also have been repeated to us younger children when we whined about having to walk a half mile to school in the cold and snowy weather. One cold snowy day, my three older siblings were warmly dressed and sent off to school, which was several miles from our house at the time. As I mentioned earlier, we had no telephone and many times not even a radio that worked.

Maybe we were just too busy and didn't have time to listen if it did work. They probably didn't broadcast school closings as much or as often back then as they do today. Anyway, they were sent off to school (walking) as usual. When they finally got to the schoolhouse, they realized school had been canceled and there was no one there. They were probably half-frozen and didn't relish a long walk back home in the cold and snow. The boys knew of a window that didn't lock, so they simply pushed it up and climbed inside. My brother, Kenny, confirmed that they turned up the heat and played school all day. Maureen was the teacher and he and Roger were the students. They had probably carried their lunch, so didn't go hungry. There was usually a big clock on the wall so they knew when it was time to go home. When it was time for school to be dismissed, they simply put on their warm wraps and made the trip back home. Mama, of course, wasn't worried about them because she just assumed they were at school as usual, not knowing it had been canceled. When she did learn about their day, I think she was very proud of them. Not many children would have been so resourceful.

I started in the second grade when we moved to May Valley. It was another two roomed school with four grades in each room. I remember one little girl who was just beginning first grade. She must never have been away from her mother much at all. When her mother would leave, this little girl began screaming and crying at the top of her lungs. Because the teacher was busy trying to console her, no teaching could take place. They would finally call her mother to come and get her. The same scenario went on for a week or more and didn't seem to be getting any better. School officials finally had to tell the mother not to bring her back that year. That family must have moved before the next school year because I don't remember seeing her again. There wasn't much movement in and out of our rural neighborhood so we mostly had the same students for all eight grades. There were a few migrant workers and other farmhands who worked for local farmers just as my father did. A few farms did sell and change ownership during those years but it was a pretty stable neighborhood.

Elementary school was mostly fun times while getting an education. We had recess every day and there was lots to do. There was the playground with swings, seesaw, monkey bars, and merry-g-round as well as a softball field and basketball hoop. Many Friday afternoons were spent in recreation, inside or out, and many times with other schools. We had spelling bees, softball games, and other fun games along with learning. Many times we would travel to other schools for competitions in these same endeavors. I was a good speller and got to represent my school in the county spelling bee competition. I was excited and proud but nervous also. I wasn't the first one to misspell a word, but I didn't get too far. I misspelled the word pedestrian.

Chicken Bristles

Christmas was always a big program time and Santa Claus paying a visit. Sometimes there would be a cake walk and/or a box supper, with boxes going to the highest bidder. We would spend time and agonize over how to decorate a box to fill with a meal. That was a scary time to see who would buy your box and who you would have to share that meal with. Mostly husbands would buy their wives box but sometimes the bidding would become very spirited between rivals or just for fun to see how high the bidder would actually go. Mrs. Guy, the upper grades teacher, was always in charge of recruiting Santa. Various fathers had the role from year to year, trying to remain anonymous for the younger children's sake since many of them still believed in Santa. We older ones were already too knowledgeable to be fooled. I remember one of the younger ones proclaiming one year, "Santa has boots just like my daddy." I'm not sure he ever really figured it out or if it was just forgotten and he never connected it again. One of the regulars that she recruited was not a parent. He was a part of our community because he owned the little country store down the road for several years. He gave everyone, and especially Mrs. Guy, a real Christman surprise one year.

He (Red) also had several brothers, one of whom did have children in our school. Red's brother lived on the outskirts of the district quite a distance from the school. Consequently. they did not interact with a lot of the neighbors. We were friends with them and knew more of their

School Days

family as well. Red played Sants for several years and many of the students never really knew who he was. Santa was always the last part of our program. Mrs. Guy would play 'Jingle Bells' on the piano as the prelude to his entrance. The year that I particularly remember, Red had played Santa for several years and didn't want the kids to get too familiar with who he was. Mrs. Guy played 'Jingle Bells'. No Santa. She played it again. No Santa. We could tell that she was beginning to get flustered as she began playing it again. Suddenly Red came in the door, wearing a green elf hat and green elf outfit. She was so surprised she actually made a mistake on that piano, something she hardly ever did. Where was Santa? She got such an astonished look on her face when Santa came in a short time later. Without her knowledge, Red had recruited one of his brothers who lived in town to fill in for him to play Santa. That would keep everyone from getting too familiar with him being our Sants Claus. The biggest joke was on Mrs. Guy. I'm not sure she ever asked him again. However, they did sell the store shortly after that and moved away.

The movie, "The Ten Commandants," took the world by storm in 1956/57. It was so popular they even scheduled an afternoon matinee during the week so school children could attend at that special time. Our school dismissed that afternoon and scheduled it as a field trip. Several of the parents drove but each student was responsible for their own admittance fee. I knew we did not have money for the movie as it was the middle of the month, between paydays. While everyone was scrambling to load into all the cars, I simply walked home since we only lived a half mile away. No sense explaining the situation. Most wouldn't understand anyway. I hadn't been home very long when one of the cars carrying students drove in. The neighbor wanted me to get in and go with them. I was so embarrassed to tell him there was no money. He just smiled and said, "We'll work it out. Just come, go with us." I will always remember the kindness of that neighbor. I really enjoyed the movie, but I don't remember much else about the afternoon.

The last day of school was always a day of fun, games, cleaning out desks, and eating. We always ended with a huge dinner on the grounds, with parents bringing their favorite dishes. Mama didn't always attend the last day of school picnic. She didn't drive, Daddy was working all day (I don't ever remember him attending one), and I sometimes think Mama was ashamed because she didn't have nice clothes. When she did come, she would either walk or catch a ride with neighbors. There was also the gossip to contend with. Mana was large and had a protruding belly. There was always the speculation, "Is Mrs. Baker expecting another baby?" We finished our school business in the morning and received our report cards. Because our dad thought so highly of education and pushed us to do well in school, we always had good grades and passed to the next higher grade with no problem. Daddy always told us, "Get a good education. That is something they can never take away from you." I think Roger was valedictorian of his eighth-grade class and I was of mine. I was the lone girl with five boys in my eighth-grade class. Now it was time to tackle high school in the big town of Lamar.

Chicken Bristles

I was very stubborn, with a mind of my own, even as a small child. In one phase of my young life, I didn't want ANYONE to mess with my hair. Of course, when there were so many children in a family, mamas didn't have time to do everything for every child. It probably fell to my older sister, Maureen, to help with my care. As older sisters go, she probably had very little patience with my screaming, kicking, twisting and turning trying to get away from her. Brushing and combing my hair in that fashion could have been rough on both of us in more ways than one. Consequently, my hair didn't get too much attention very often. I was perfectly happy with that. Of course, that didn't do much for my appearance either. If you can imagine a three to-five-year-old child who spent most of her time running wild, playing outside in the dirt and muck, you can probably imagine what my hair looked like. It was long, dirty, string, and sticking up and out every which way.

Chicken Bristles

My brothers and sister started calling me 'chicken bristles.' I probably looked like one of those old hens who was puffed up all over and ready for battle. I even threw a fit when Mama tried to wash my hair. I didn't mind what they called me as long as they didn't mess with my hair.

Daddy worked six days a week and had Sundays off as long as there was no irrigation water. Sometimes he would spend Sunday afternoon brushing my hair. Since I was a Daddy's girl and he was so patient and gentle, I would allow him to brush and comb my hair, but he was the only one who could do it. I distinctly remember one Sunday afternoon when Maureen was again delegated to brush my hair. Naturally I was throwing my usual fit, yelling "I want Daddy to do it. I want Daddy to do it." When I saw Daddy come out of the house, I just knew I had gotten what I wanted. To my utter surprise and shock, he grabbed that hairbrush out of Maureen's hand, turned me over and swatted my behind with it. He said, "I'm tired. I've been up all night irrigating and am trying to get a little sleep. Now stop that yelling and let Maureen brush your hair." Then he stormed back into the house. I probably whimpered and sniffled some, but I let Maureen brush my hair. That is one of the few, if any, times I remember getting a spanking from my father.

Back then it wasn't as easy to wash hair or take a bath as it is today. We couldn't just stand under a shower or over a sink with running water. Water for anything had to be drawn from the cistern and heated on the wood-burning stove if we wanted it hot. That was hard labor in itself so we didn't do it any more than necessary. Our bath and hair washing were usually done weekly. We had a round, galvanized tub that we carried into the kitchen, as that was the warmest room, especially in the winter. In summer, we sometimes could move to the enclosed back porch. We didn't all get clean water. Usually two or three would bathe before the water was emptied and the tub refilled. The cleanest ones got to bathe first. I don't think I was overly fond of baths either until I started school and wanted to be clean. Until then I never went anywhere very often, so why do all that cleaning up?

I don't think Mama was much good at fixing hair. In later years, she always wore hers short and straight to save time and avoid having to do anything with it. She just had to run a comb through it and she was ready to go. When I was younger, it was long and she kept it braided and piled atop her head. I think Mama tried to fix mine, but just didn't know how to fix hair all that well. Looking at some of my elementary school pictures, I still had a lot of that 'chicken bristle' look. I probably tried to fix my own hair but didn't do too good a job as I was still in the learning process.

Chicken Bristles

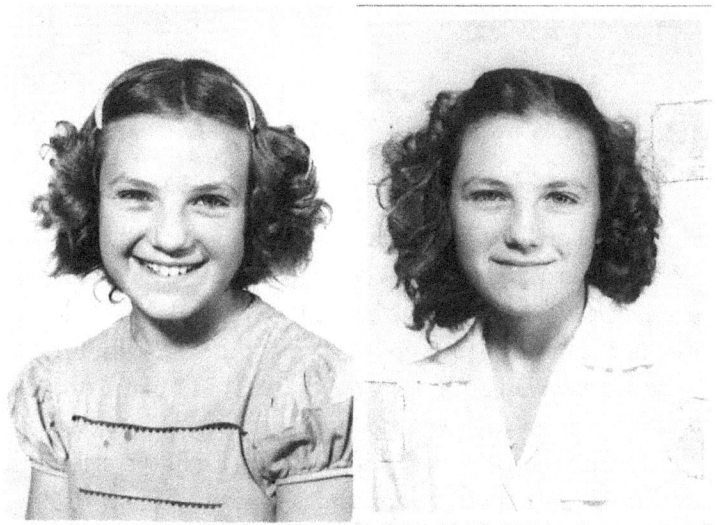

Even in later school years on picture taking day, I still
had some of that 'chicken bristles' look.

Mama did do my hair up in rag curls sometimes, but the curl didn't last long. I still don't like messing with my hair and wear a curly perm most of the time. I just run a comb through it and I'm good to go. There are more important things to do in life than messing with my hair.

Lost

*P*ayday for Daddy was once a month. The Saturday after payday was when we went to town for groceries. Us kids got to go to the show (movie). Very seldom did all the family get to go to town at the same time. There were too many in our family for all of us to fit in the car and still have room for the groceries later. Daddy was the one who did all the grocery shopping. I don't remember Mama ever doing much of it. Sometimes she would go with him, but Daddy was the shopper. Mama would give him a list of the staples we needed and he would fill in with other things he thought we needed. After the trip to the grocery store, it was time for us kids to go to the show. Daddy would sometimes go to the café for a steak dinner and then to the tavern for a beer or two. He didn't drink much, but went more for the conversation while he waited for us to get out of the show. He sure didn't drink enough to get drunk, as he knew he would have all of us in the car with him on his

Lost

way back home. The conversation and companionship were more important to him. Because he worked such long hard hours, there wasn't a lot of time to visit with other men. He had to take advantage when he could.

One Saturday night, maybe before I had started school, we went as usual to the show. It was only Kenny, Roger and me on this trip. When we left the theater, Kenny and Roger ran ahead of me and got to the tavern first. I guess I was too far behind them and didn't see exactly which building they entered. Since I wasn't sure where they were, I just kept walking. Main street was very long and the railroad divided it into north and south Main. We usually only frequented south of the tracks because that was the nicer part of town. I knew about the seedier part of town but wasn't that familiar with all the businesses on that end. After a bad section, there were more desirable businesses. I walked through the bad part and then into the better part, still not knowing where Daddy and the boys were. After a while I noticed a young couple following me. They followed me for several blocks and finally asked me, "Little girl, are you lost?" I explained why I was where I was. They offered to help me find my family. I knew the approximate area where Daddy usually parked to wait for us, so that was where we headed. I had no recourse but to trust that they would help me. They didn't have a vehicle so we had to walk back to that area. Sure enough, there were my Daddy and brothers, frantic with worry about where I might be. I don't think they had gotten too far looking for me yet, as they really didn't know where to search. They had probably retraced the route to the theater and were trying to decide what to do next.

Main street of Lamar was strung out along either side of highway 50. At the northern edge of town, several more blocks north of where the couple found me, was a big ditch, known simply as the Lamar ditch. I had no idea where the water in it came from or where it went. It was usually full of water and running swiftly. It was probably part of the Amity canal irrigation system. When we got to where Daddy and the boys were, this couple told Daddy about finding me and offering to help me find them. Everything was going as it should until they told Daddy they had found me playing around the Lamar ditch, leaning over and throwing rocks and sticks into it. I was shocked! I had been nowhere near that ditch, even several blocks away from it. I'm not sure if Daddy believed them or me. After all, they were the adults and I was only a child. I know that I protested that I had been nowhere near that ditch. I don't think I got into any trouble over the incident. Maybe Daddy reprimanded the boys for not keeping better track of me. Daddy was just glad I had been found and was not injured in any way. Even today when I drive down that Main Street, I can still pinpoint almost the exact spot where I was. Still nowhere near the Lamar ditch. It upset me to have them lie to my dad that way. Looking back on the incident as an adult, I figured maybe it just made them seem more heroic to have rescued me from a possible death from drowning. That incident probably began to form my distrust of people, which still persists to some degree today. I know the incident is lodged very firmly in my mind.

Wild (?) Animals

*N*o matter where we lived, we always had animals around, even if they weren't all pets. There were chickens, dogs, cats and usually sheep and/or pigs. Most of the farmers Daddy worked for raised a few sheep, especially in the winter months when there wasn't much else going on. They had to make their employee earn his pay somehow, plus it gave them some extra income. Many times, we got the orphan lambs to feed and raise because they had to be bottle fed. The farmers didn't like to take the time and trouble to mess with them. The pigs consumed the slop that came from discarded peelings, spoiled food, etc. We also bought some feed and mixed mash for them. The pigs had to be kept penned up, but the sheep sometimes had the run of the yard. They were also fun to play with and we treated them like pets. The chickens were also allowed to roam free most of the time. We tried to keep them in the coop at night so other animals didn't snatch them to eat. We had

hens to lay eggs and roosters to strut and keep the hens in line. When the hens got too old to lay eggs, they made fine eating, either fried or stewed as chicken and noodles or dumplings. We usually bought flour in twenty- five- pound bags, so we ate lots of biscuits and gravy and noodles or dumplings. Along with pinto beans, these were the staple foods at our house.

Chickens could also be made into pets. Most of them weren't afraid of us and would come running when we had something to feed them. Some of the roosters could be mean. We had one who seemed to delight in chasing me whenever I went into the yard. I tried to stay out of his way as much as possible. If he saw me outside, he would run at me and flog my legs. I was terrified of him. We also had one sheep that took delight in butting me every chance he got. I could go out to play more when the older kids were around because they would keep both animals away from me. They were my protectors.

Killing a chicken to eat was not my job: usually my mother took care of that chore. I did have to help run them down and catch them for the killing. Mama knew how to wring their neck so no blood was shed. Since she was home more than anyone else, she did most of the chicken killing. I guess I just got used to her way of killing and didn't think too much about any other way. Once when I was still quite small, Daddy and the boys were tasked with killing some chickens. Of course, being more manly, they used the axe to cut off their heads. I had never seen them killed that way before. Because I always had to be in on what my brothers were doing, I was right there watching the process. Even with their head cut off and turned loose, those old chickens did a lot of flopping around before they died completely, and blood was flying everywhere. I was close enough that some of the blood landed on my legs. Besides never having seen such a spectacle before, I don't think I had ever had blood like that on me before. I ran screaming to the house, burst in and grabbed some old newspapers and started piling them on my legs to cover the blood. I kept screaming, "He bleeded on me. He bleeded on me." Mama had quite a time getting me calmed down so she could wash the blood off me. There probably wasn't that much blood and wasn't nearly as much of a big deal as I made it out to be, but I wasn't a fan of watching chickens killed again either. It was bad enough that I had to help pull the feathers off after they had been scalded. An even worse task was pulling out the insides of a dead chicken. Mama handled that job as well as I hated to do it.

We had one large, older sheep that roamed all around the yard and got to be quite tame. We had a cistern for our water everywhere we lived. They all had a large opening at the top so we could let the buckets down and draw the water out. The opening was kept covered so no one could fall in, but the cover could be easily moved when we needed to draw water or clean the cistern out. One day, we could not find our sheep, but we could hear him bleating. After searching for quite a while, we saw that the boards covering the cistern opening had been moved aside. Trying to discover what had knocked them askew, we saw that old sheep swimming around down in the water. Somehow, he had kicked the covering aside and fallen in. What a mess! How were we going to get him out? It was not an easy job. He weighed quite a bit and was even heavier with his wool full of water. I think they had to use a tractor. Someone had to go into the cistern and tie a rope around him in order to pull him up. They did get him out alive, but he didn't get to stay around long after that. Off to market he went. Of course, all the water in the cistern had been contaminated. We had to draw it all out, dispose of it, then go down and scrub the entire cistern before we could get a new truckload of water. The opening was kept more secure after that.

Is that a bear? When we lived at Channing, there was a small creek about a half mile or so from our house. We four older kids liked to play there, catching what we called crawdads. I don't know whether they were actually crawdads or just tadpoles, but it was great fun anyway. We had probably been told many times to be home before dark, but as kids tend to do, there were many times when it was after dark when we got back to the house. One evening that I remember, we got involved in the creek as we usually did, and darkness was upon us before we realized it and started toward home. The road we had to travel was parallel to the railroad tracks. We lived on the other side of those tracks so had to cross over them to get to our house. As we walked along, chattering and carrying on, one of us glanced up and saw something walking along the railroad tracks. It seemed to be walking on all fours and just looked like a big lump lumbering along. We had no idea what it was other than a silhouette in the semi-darkness. It also seemed to be keeping pace with us. We walked. It walked. We stopped. It stopped. What could it be? We didn't know if there were bears in that area, but it sure looked like a small bear to us. We kept walking. So did that thing. When we stopped, it did too. We were getting more scared by the minute. We still had to cross those tracks to get home. Would it attack us? Could we run fast enough to escape it? Nothing else to do. We just kept walking and watching. Suddenly it disappeared. That's when we really began to get scared. We had no idea where it had gone or whether it was simply waiting for us to cross the tracks. Would it attack us there? Could we outrun it and get to the house safely? Since we couldn't see it anymore, we simply made a mad dash for the house. We surely were four scared kids when we reached the house. We also had to explain, again, why we were late getting home, but we were eager, scared and excited to tell our story about the thing (a wild animal?) that had shadowed and stalked us most of the way home. It was much later that we found out our wild animal had actually been our mother. She had put on an old, bulky overcoat, and sneaked down along the tracks until she heard us coming on the road. She simply bent over and followed along the tracks with us. She probably thought it would teach us a good lesson about staying out after dark. We had certainly been scared out of our wits for a time. I don't think we realized what a sense of humor she had. She thought it had been great fun and laughed about it for years.

Another time she had us scared because we thought she had run away and left us. I don't remember where we had been, but it was outside somewhere. When we came into the house, there was no Mama waiting for us. We called out for her several times, but there was no answer. We started searching the house. I think Ruby was the baby and she was still in her crib. "Surely she wouldn't go away and leave the baby behind". That was the tone of our questions, but where could she be? She was always there, didn't know how to drive, so how could she go? I think we were really starting to get scared and actually started crying when she appeared from wherever she had been hiding. She laughed and thought it was a great joke on us. We tried to stay a little closer to home, at least for a while, after that. We really did not want her to disappear out of our lives. She did not leave the farm very often and probably had to liven things up a little to help keep her sanity. She surely did not have an easy life.

Chicken Bristles

I can't remember if we always had a dog, but I can remember a couple of them. One was a big black (I think) one. I don't remember much about him except that he began to chase sheep, which was a big no-no for a farmer who raised sheep. We tried keeping him penned up in the chicken pen after that happened, but that only seemed to make him mean. He would try to bite us if we came close enough to pet him. The only thing left to do was get rid of him by putting him down. Daddy and the boss were going to shoot him. Daddy gave us instructions to stay in the house and away from the window so we didn't have to watch it. For some reason I happened to go out the back door and had just started around the house when he was shot. I knew it had to be done, so it wasn't as traumatic as it could have been otherwise. It was a long time before we had another dog though.

The other dog I remember was a smaller, brown and white one of mixed breeds. We got him from my cousin, Charles, so he was named Chuckie. He was a very friendly dog and got along well with all of us. He was something of a scaredy cat though. Whenever someone would drive into our yard, under the porch he would run to hide. From the safety of his hiding place, he would bark like crazy. Just to listen to him, he was a very ferocious dog. He wouldn't come out of there easily until the danger was gone. I don't know how long he lived, but he was still there when I left home. We seemed to have cats and even a white rabbit once.

Wild (?) Animals

We didn't know for sure whatever happened to that rabbit. He got out of his cage somehow and ran away. All we ever found was a lot of white fur bits in a hay field after it had been mowed. We weren't sure whether it was an animal that got him or if he got caught in the mower.

Flood

The Amity ditch/canal carried a lot of water which supplied the local farmers with their irrigation water. The system was a wonderful necessity for the dry lands of southeastern Colorado. It was well controlled and went where it was directed.

Flood

Amity headgate: irrigation water
dispersed to each district from here.

However, once there was a major problem. We lived on the lower side of the ditch at that time. One night we awoke with water running through the house. We had had no rain, so where was it coming from? My dad was pretty smart about a lot of things. I don't think it took him very long to realize that there had been a break in that huge ditch. I was so young I can't remember a lot of details. I know it was a scary time. I was being pulled some and carried some to somewhere (?) and up over or onto the railroad tracks. I don't remember where we went, or what else happened. I just remember I was scared of all that water. That's probably why I have had some fear of water all my life. There is no recollection of how long the water ran free before someone got to the main switch and diverted it elsewhere. Nor do I have any idea how long it took to get it repaired. As far as I know, it has never broken again and that has been many years ago. Once was enough. The farmhouse we lived in at the time was probably rendered unlivable with all that water running through it. It probably was not in the best of condition before that even happened. That could have been the reason we moved to another house in another school district. The farmers my dad worked for were not known for their generosity in providing well for their workers. That one probably didn't want to repair the house.

Pickup Adventures

We had a car, but it was old and not always operable and Daddy couldn't afford repairs on it. It remained parked out back under a tree until Daddy bought a newer one. The boss provided a pickup for Daddy to drive which ensured he was able to get back and forth to whichever field he was working in. Many times, it was our only means of transportation. I don't think the boss really minded that we drove it for personal reasons as he didn't pay that well. It was more than likely simply considered as part of the salary package. He was well aware that my dad was an excellent farm hand so he wanted to keep him satisfied.

Daddy drove us many places in that pickup even though it probably was not always the same one. I'm sure they wore

out and the boss did not supply expensive equipment that would last a long time. Not one vehicle stands out as special. There was just always one available. They didn't have the big double cabs back then like they do now. Consequently, because of our large family, there wasn't room in the cab for everyone. Us kids loved that because it meant we got to ride in the back when the whole family went somewhere. Saturday night grocery shopping meant everyone didn't always get to go. If they did, we got to ride in the back. It wasn't so much fun during cold weather, but we would bundle up with coats and blankets to brave the elements. It was much nicer to ride back there during warmer weather. That kind of travel could get folks in lots of trouble today.

Daddy had a sister who lived in Syracuse, Kansas, with her family. That was about fifty miles from where we lived. When we took the pickup and went to visit, Mama would usually ride along to visit with the family. That meant us kids got to ride in the back of the truck. Between our place and theirs was an abandoned Japanese detention camp named Camp Amache. Daddy would sometimes take a detour down the side road just to see what remained of it. Our family came to that area in 1945 or 1946, so it might have been still open and operating then. Daddy was probably very familiar with it because of that. He just liked to keep in touch with it.

Pickup Adventures

Construction of the camp was started in June, 1942, and was officially closed January 27, 1945, after all the detainees had been released or relocated. It was quite a place in its heyday, the tenth largest city in Colorado at the time. Everything a regular city would have was included in it: post office, hospital, schools, as well as barracks for living, a recreation hall, laundry, toilet, and shower rooms. There was also a certain amount of freedom, as detainees could walk into Granada for a variety of shopping. Many of its 10,500 acres were used for agriculture. It was almost self-sustaining and much of its surplus was sent to help sustain other camps. There were ten of these camps scattered among Utah, Arizona, Wyoming, Arkansas, Idaho, Colorado and California. I think Amache was actually the smallest, a piece of history that should never have happened. It was a terrible misjustice to a race of people simply because of fear. While in a high school English class, I came across a book about two teenagers who lived in that camp and gave a book report on it. Most of my fellow classmates had never even heard of it, let alone knew it was so close to Lamar. Except for my dad's interest in it, I might not have heard of it either. When the camp closed, most of the buildings were torn down immediately and all of them were torn down eventually. My daughter and I stopped by there once when we were on vacation. There was nothing left except foundations and emptiness. I think they have now started rebuilding some of the buildings to create a museum. It has also been placed on the National Historical Registry. I'd like to go back someday to see what has been restored. It's a piece of history that should not be forgotten.

At least once that I can remember, we got into trouble when we were riding in the back of the pickup. If I remember correctly, it was Kenny, Roger and me in the back. We were blessed in that part of the country with many cottonwood trees. Spring had arrived and the trees were loaded with those hard little cotton balls that would later turn to cottonwood fluff. Did it matter where we were headed, either to Syracuse or Camp Amache? It was on that stretch of highway that could have been either one. The pickup bed was covered with all those little balls. What a bright idea we had! It seemed like it would be fun to throw those little balls at things as we were riding along down the highway. Of course, they hit some of the cars and bounced off. No harm done. They were soft and couldn't hurt anything. One lady got mad when a few of them hit her windshield. She thought we were throwing rocks at her. Flagging our truck down, she proceeded to lecture my dad about his naughty children throwing rocks at people. Why, one of them could have come right through her windshield and someone could have been seriously injured or caused a wreck. I think Daddy believed us about only throwing cotton balls, as there were still lots of them left. A good lecture was forthcoming, maybe more for her benefit than ours. I don't remember getting into any other trouble about it. We didn't throw any more that trip, but we laughed about it for a long time. Who would have thought they were rocks anyway?

Wood was our major source of heating and cooking, which meant we had to have a steady supply of wood handy. We had some trees nearby that could be cut up to burn, but most had to come from farther away. Usually, we would go elsewhere, fill the back of the truck and deliver it to our yard. We could finish cutting it to size when we got it home. Once or twice, I remember Daddy dragging an entire tree home, down the gravel road from several miles away. How the dust would fly! It was quicker to get it home that way. We could saw it into smaller logs as it was needed. We had a long crosscut saw that took two of us at a time to operate it. All of us got our turn on one end of it. After sawing it into logs, it then had to be split into smaller chunks with the axe in order to fit into the stoves. We all had to take our turn with that, too. We didn't have any major accidents with the saw or axe. In later years, Mama did lose part of one finger by getting too close to the sawblade. Exercise wasn't a word in our vocabulary as something to do. We had plenty of it just staying busy and living.

We traveled many miles in those old pickups until daddy traded in his old Ford for a newer used car that we could all ride in at one time. Maureen had left home by then, so there were fewer of us to actually ride in it. The pickup still came in handy for a multitude of tasks. It was useful for hauling

Chicken Bristles

livestock to the county fair, dragging trees home to cut up for firewood and just all around traveling somewhere. Only fond memories come to mind about pickups. I would still like to own one, as it could come in handy even today.

Bullies

Long before it was widely acknowledged, there were bullies. Our community had two of them and I seemed to be one of their prime targets. It wasn't constant, but I knew I bore the brunt of their petty meanness. Larry and Keith were three or four years older than me, placing them in age between Roger and Kenny. My two older brothers were friends with everyone, so they didn't have any trouble. Pinches, pokes, stares, tripping and other petty hassles were mine to endure. These hassles weren't done openly for others to see. They were much too wise for that, for they knew they could get into trouble. Having to stand in front of them during our program practices could be a nightmare: pinches on the butt, pokes, sly whispers and such were normal from them. I was victim of several trippings that sent me sprawling. One day when I was in the fourth grade, the upper grade teacher, Mrs. Guy, came into our room with Larry in tow. She said to our teacher loud

enough for all to hear her, "I think one of my boys owes one of your girls an apology." I had no idea that girl was me, so wasn't sure what he should be apologizing for. I was certainly surprised when he walked over to my desk and said, "I'm sorry." Even then, I didn't know what the problem was until Mrs. Guy explained. "I was looking out my window yesterday as the students were leaving, and I saw this big boy tripping this young girl. I thought he should have to apologize in front of everyone because he should be ashamed of himself." I was glad she gave that explanation because it was such a normal thing that I had almost forgotten about it. It also let them know that I had not snitched on them. That would have increased the abuse and/or made it worse.

Another time I got tripped was during a ball game. Many of our Friday afternoons during nice weather, we traveled to other schools for ball games, spelling bees and other activities. This particular afternoon, we had traveled to Clover Meadow school for an afternoon of playing ball. I'm not sure if there were other schools that had also been invited. Keith was on the opposite team and was the second baseman. As I approached his base, running hard, he put out his foot and tripped me. I surely did go flying into second base, just not the way I had planned. Of course, everyone simply thought I had stumbled since no one saw him do it. It was a gravel field and some of the gravel was embedded in my skinned arms and legs. The teachers probably washed and treated my scrapes, but they weren't that serious and the game continued. I had to tell Mama and Daddy what had happened, but it wasn't enough of a big deal to cause trouble over. We didn't make waves over something that trivial since we had to live and get along in our community. I learned to live with it.

I don't think it was ever proven, but I also think they were responsible for destroying out melon patch one year. Our big vegetable garden was in one area and the melon patch in another location. It was a huge area in a field next to the road, large enough for all the melon, cucumber and often pumpkin vines to spread out. That particular year, we had a really good crop of watermelons and cantaloupes. They were ripe and ready to pick. We just hadn't gotten to them yet. One morning when we went out to check on them, almost all of them had been slashed to pieces. We were able to salvage a small portion so they wouldn't all go to waste. It was just such a senseless waste of good food that we had spent time and effort on. I always suspected it was the two of them, but once again, nothing could be proven. I don't remember anything being said about it later or anyone getting into trouble over it. However, as a youngster, I wasn't privy to everything that went on. My two bullies graduated from May Valley and went on to high school years before I did. My last two years at May Valley were a lot more peaceful with them gone. High school was a much larger school, so I didn't have to put up with them. They had better things to do by then. I think we did ride the school bus together some, but I don't recall any problems with them on the bus. Life became easier and more pleasant without their meanness.

Music

Music, in some fashion, was always a part on our lives. We had an old upright piano that had been with Mama and Daddy since their marriage. It was always part of my life. Mama knew how to pick out a few keys, but did not really know how to play. She would sit down and pick out a few notes of "Beulah Land" when she had a little extra time. She especially liked that song because it was her name. She would have liked one of us kids to learn to play it, but we never did. We had a neighbor lady who offered to teach Ruby and me how to play if we would come to her house. The problem was that she lived a long two or more miles from us and we had to walk. After taking a few lessons, we lost interest and disliked the long walk even more. While doing some cleaning and sorting just recently, I discovered my old music book that I didn't even realize I had kept.

Chicken Bristles

In the upper grades at May Valley, we had to learn how to play an instrument which we called a flute. Many years later, I learned it was actually called a recorder. Some elementary schools still use them in their music programs, I learned. When visiting a friend in Washington, DC, in later years, I learned that she belonged to a recorder group. She told me that many of the members still played the little recorder like we used while some others owned more expensive ones; some even worth thousands of dollars. Ours was always just the simple hard plastic one. Any program that we had at school always included our flute band. Mrs. Guy, our teacher, would write the notes on the blackboard and we would learn to play as a group, memorizing the notes. After graduating from eighth grade, we had no further use for it so the flute was handed down to the next in line. In recent years, one of our elementary students at church played a Christmas special on one. Rediscovering them, I stopped at a music store and purchased one. I may even learn to play it again someday.

We didn't always own a radio that actually played. When we did have one, it was used by the whole family for news and some of the programs popular during that time. 'The Lone Ranger' was us kids favorite while Mama liked 'Fibber McGee and Molly.' I think we somehow acquired a battery-powered radio because I can remember taking it outside when the weather was nice and hooking the antenna onto the metal clothesline so it would pick up

Music

'The Grand Ole Opry' on Saturday nights. We liked our country music. Daddy had some Hank Snow records that we played as long as the Victrola or record player worked. Country music is still my favorite, but I mostly stick to the older songs and artists. I liked to sing and was a member of chorus in high school. Varsity Chorus was composed of those chosen by try out. I was never fortunate enough to make it into that, as much as I wanted to. I came very close my senior year except they did not increase the number of students involved which would have included new members. I still like to sing but the voice is just not what it used to be. Now I just make a 'joyful noise to the Lord'.

New Dress

Most of our clothes were hand-me-downs, were given to us used or came from thrift stores. We hardly knew what new outer clothes were. An aunt who lived in California would send us a box of used clothes every year around Christmas. We were always excited to get it and whenever it arrived was Christmas for us. We checked it out thoroughly to discover all the goodies and treasures it contained. Next came deciding what would fit who and distribute it accordingly. The Spiegel catalog was the source of most of our new socks and underwear, mostly around the new school year or Christmas, maybe as birthday presents. Receiving that catalog in the mail was a special time. We spent many hours turning pages, making a list and dreaming about what we might actually get. We had to be content with what we did get, mostly basic stuff.

New Dress

I don't remember getting any new clothes from a store in town in my early years. We bought sugar and flour sometimes in twenty-five or fifty-pound cloth bags, as well as chicken and hog feed. Mama did make me a simple feed sack dress from them a time or two. Mostly I just wore hand-me-downs from my older sister and brothers. Occasionally, I even had to wear my brothers' shoes because we simply could not afford new ones for all of us. That was embarrassing but necessary.

I remember the thrill I got from my first new dress, from an actual dress store. Sherry was a baby so I was around nine or ten. The local radio station was running a contest for Mother's Day. The contestants had to write a short essay about something to do with mothers; I don't remember exactly what. Mama urged me to write something and send in an entry. I think I wrote something about helping my mother take care of my baby sister. Whatever I wrote, it was chosen as the winning entry. My prize was an article of clothing from a store in town. Thrilling! Exciting! I really did get to go in and choose something for my very own, not just look and dream. I proudly wore the dress I chose as long as I possible could. I don't remember getting many more new dresses throughout grade school until eighth grade graduation. I don't remember where I got it, but it didn't hold near the excitement as that first new dress as a younger child.

Chicken Bristles

Another new dress for eighth grade graduation.
Me with my four male classmates

Even today I am very careful with my clothes and have a tendency to keep them a long time. Just recently, my daughter was admiring whatever I was wearing. When I commented that I had had it for a long time, she said, "Mother, everything you've got, you've had for a long time." Why spend money for something new when the old is still good?

Outhouse
And *Cistern*

As a child, it was never my privilege to live in a house with any type of indoor plumbing. We had an outhouse, usually a two-holer, and a cistern. We never had a well or pump; it was a cistern that we had to manually draw water from. Water was delivered to our cistern by truck from a large commercial well. The hole for the outhouse was hand dug and the little building placed over it. When a hole got full, another was dug and the building moved. If it was deep enough, it tended to be useful for years. Modern toilet paper was not a luxury we were allowed or could afford. When we had exhausted wishing from the latest catalog received in the mail, it was relegated to the outhouse as wiping material. A mite rougher than today's toilet paper, but it did the job. Those houses were hot in the summer

and cold in the winter. We frequently kept a bucket somewhere in the house, especially in winter, to avoid that trek out in the cold. Sometimes, the little house was closer than others and wasn't quite so bad. One place where we lived, the outhouse was quite a distance from the living quarters. There was tall grassy patch between the two that we had to travel to get to the outhouse. My oldest brother, Kenny, was scared of the dark and hated to make that trip after dark. When he had to make that trip at night before bedtime, he would push me down the path in front of him. He rationalized that if the bogey man jumped out and got me, he could run back to the house for safety. Maybe the bogey man was scared of both of us because he never jumped out to catch either of us. We had to share the outhouse with all kinds of bugs and spiders, once in a while even a snake. That was scary enough.

The boss did not upgrade the house at May Valley with indoor plumbing until well after I had graduated from high school and left home. I think some of the neighbors shamed him into it. They would drive past and see my mother out digging another hole so the outhouse could be moved. When he remodeled and installed indoor water and plumbing, she ended up using that hole for trash. There had been two bedrooms downstairs, so one of them was converted into a bathroom and laundry room with not much trouble. We had always used a wringer washing machine which sat on our partially enclosed back porch. We had to

Outhouse And Cistern

draw water from the cistern and heat it on the wood cook stove which made it quite laborious. Drying the clothes was accomplished by hanging everything on a clothesline outside. Mama and Daddy were finally able to have a modern washer and dryer. I'm not sure if Sherry was still living at home when all that took place. After Mama got sick and was not able to do much of anything, Daddy was able to keep the laundry done because he had those nice machines. When we went home to visit, it was nice for us kids to be able to use a nice indoor bathroom like we were used to by now.

The cisterns were usually quite large. The one the sheep fell into had to be large enough for him to be able to swim around in even though the memory of it is vague. I know the one at May Valley seemed to be huge. It was probably six to eight or ten feet across and at least that deep. It probably seemed much larger at the time because I was the one chosen to be let down into it when it was time to be cleaned. It had a cement floor and the sides were a combination of cement and rocks. Not an easy job, especially for a child. We didn't clean it between every load; just often enough to keep the water fairly clean. After all, that was what we drank and cooked with, as well as bathe in and do laundry. A fair share of bugs and such died in there. I was big enough to clean and small enough to be let down in a bucket to mop up all the excess water, along with all the mud and bugs, before we could get a new load delivered. The boys would lower me down in a bucket, which I would fill with muck, and they would draw it back up and dispose of it. This was repeated until the cistern was clean. After it was cleaned, they would taunt me and threaten to leave me down there until the load of water was delivered. The water hauler served the whole community, so we had to schedule when our water would be delivered and tried to clean it the day before, storing enough water to last until he could get there. We had to clean it at least once, maybe twice each year. Another one of those jobs not really pleasant, but necessary for our good health.

Vacation

Family vacation was not a yearly experience at our house. I can remember only one in all my years growing up. We just did not have the means, time or money, to do so. Daddy worked long and hard hours. I'm not sure he even got vacation time, even though he worked for the same man for many years. The one vacation that I can remember was taken when I was around six or seven. It may have been a time when Daddy was between jobs and actually had some free time. We traveled light and did not indulge in paying for sleeping rooms at night. Roy was the youngest, so there would have been eight of us in Daddy's old Ford when we left Colorado and headed for Nebraska. Mama had at least one sister and other relatives living there and that was our destination. It was a different time and life was much simpler back then. When we got tired of traveling and needed rest, Daddy pulled to the side of a road, we threw our blankets on the ground and spent the night. We carried most of

Chicken Bristles

our food with us, so we didn't have to spend much on meals along the way. Of course, we couldn't travel as fast back then as we do today. It probably took at least a couple of days to get to Nebraska.

We made it to our destination, Falls City, Nebraska, and spent several days there. About all I remember of that time is being in a back yard with Ruby and I cuddling on a blanket while the adults visited. There were several relatives to visit before we headed for Missouri to visit some of Daddy's relatives. Once while traveling down the highway on our way to Missouri, we came over a hill and the road was covered in water. I was scared but Daddy just kept driving as it didn't seem to be moving. Thinking back on it now, it may have just been the way the sun was shining on the roadway and it wasn't really water at all. Funny how our minds can play tricks on us. Daddy's sister, Jean, lived out in the country with her large family. My brother told me he did remember that it had been raining and we had to cross a creek on the way to their house. The water in the creek was higher than usual and we almost didn't make it out as the opposite bank was very slippery. I don't remember much about that visit except that we again spent several days. Then, we were homeward bound, traveling much the same as we did at the beginning. That was the one and only vacation I remember taking as a family. If we went anywhere, it was usually just to an aunt or uncle's house for a Sunday afternoon visit since that was the only day Daddy had off.

Vacation

Even those visits were few and far between. My grandfather on Daddy's side lived with one of Daddy's brothers for a time, on a farm near Lamar. I remember visiting him only a time or two. All I can really remember about my grandfather was that he had a big black mole on his face and had to spend a lot of time in bed. He died while I was still quite young. He is buried in Missouri, so Daddy probably went back to his funeral on the train. I do remember him being gone for a few days several times, but didn't really know all the whys or where he went.

Many years after my husband died and I was living with my daughter, we finally made it to the family reunion on Daddy's mother's side of the family, the Bethels. I met relatives I didn't even know about. Some of the cousins who were at that reunion were from Aunt Jean's family that we had visited so long ago on our vacation. They were all younger than me and didn't remember our visit. They did remember my dad visiting their mother at a later date, maybe more than once. Maybe he had gone by train to the annual Bethel reunion and I just wasn't aware of it. They all made it a point to tell me (and a brother at a later reunion) how my dad and their mother would sit up until all hours of the night visiting and laughing. They would then be up early the next morning and start all over again. I learned from some of the other relatives about one of the times Daddy had gone to Missouri. It was when his grandmother died. His mother died when he was a teenager. When he went

Chicken Bristles

back for his grandmother's funeral, the train station where he had to get off was seven miles from where the funeral was to be held. In order to make it to the funeral on time, he had to run those seven miles. Of course, he was all hot, sweaty and dirty. The other relatives managed to get him washed and into some clean clothes before the funeral. Times surely were a lot different back then.

Tumbleweed Christmas

Christmas was not a huge celebration at our house. We usually got a few gifts, like socks and underwear, from the Spiegel catalog. If times were good, there might also be some kind of toy or other goodies. If we had a tree, it was most often the cast-off from school which had been undecorated and would be tossed out before Christmas vacation began. We kept ornaments from year to year so we didn't have to worry about buying them each year. Christmas was usually just another day and a vacation from school. Daddy probably even got the day off after animals were fed. My most memorable Christmas was the year we lived in the Carlton district. I think Daddy had lost his job with one farmer and began working for another one who didn't have a house available for us. He did have two abandoned houses

Chicken Bristles

sitting side by side that had been used for chickens. I went with my mother to clean them up before we could move in. We had to literally scoop out the dried chicken poop and bedding, plus scrub it thoroughly, before we were able to live there. One house alone was not large enough to house all of us as well as belongings. We cooked, ate and used one as the living quarters and sleeping rooms for my parents and the younger children. The older ones slept in the other house and some of our belongings were also stored in it. I think I remember sleeping in both at one time or another. The time spent living there was some of the hardest I can remember. I know we didn't spend a full year there. It was probably from late fall to late spring of the next year but we were there for a memorable Christmas.

We didn't have a tree that year, even from the school. Someone else spoke for it first. We knew times were hard for our folks so we were resigned to not having a tree that year. We knew we were lucky to have a place to live and food to eat, even if it was also scarce at times. Since we lived on the dry plains, there were always tumbleweeds blowing with the wind and getting stuck in fence rows. My resourceful mother just went to the back fence and rescued one of the huge weeds caught there. Since we had our ornaments and tinsel from previous years, all we had to do was decorate it. No lights, maybe some popcorn to string and put on it and that tumbleweed made a delightful substitute. Everything may not have been exactly as I remember it but I remember it very fondly.

Food was also in short supply that year and there was very little for Christmas dinner. We didn't even have any chickens left to kill. We got our mail at the little country store and combination post office about a half mile up the road. Mama sent us there the day before Christmas to see if we had gotten any mail. We did! There was a letter from an aunt, which we promptly delivered to Mama. That letter contained FIVE dollars: much needed money. Mama sent us right back to the store to buy our Christmas dinner. We dined very well that Christmas on beans and cornbread. We survived the holidays and the worst time with thanksgiving. Better times would come after we moved to May Valley in the new year.

Church

Attendance at church was not a regular occurrence as I was growing up. Mama didn't drive and Daddy was usually working or too tired to take us. The only church nearby was after we moved to May Valley. Mama was raised in the Congregational church but since there wasn't one of those close, she didn't care where we attended. There was a small community church several miles from our house that most in the community attended. It was officially named the Church of God Bethel, but everyone just called it Clover Meadow church, since it was in that district. We were dependent on neighbors to take us when we wanted to go or when they offered us a ride. One neighbor in particular took us quite regularly since she drove right past our house anyway. We always attended Vacation Bible School in the summer as did most of the other neighborhood kids. It probably got everybody out of their parents' hair for a few hours a day for two weeks during summer vacation. It was

Church

always a lot of fun but was limited to certain grades/ages. The Sunday after it ended, we usually put on some kind of program about what we learned and then had dinner on the grounds. Everyone brought something to eat, which was done outside. We played games and visited until later in the afternoon. Always a fun time.

There was one particular lady who lived in town but attended that church. She was a very stern type lady: my brothers did not like her at all and tried to avoid her whenever possible. I didn't mind her even though she could be quite forceful at times. She was instrumental in getting me to join the WCTU (Women's Christian Temperance Union). I wasn't involved much but it probably did have a profound influence on my life. I attended church sporadically at Clover Meadow until high school. I don't remember when it closed, but it was closed for many years and eventually torn down. There was only an empty lot for a long time until someone built a house on it. Clover Meadow school was across the road and I think it has even been torn down by now. Only the memories live on.

It was in my later high school years that I actually gave my life to Christ after I started attending the Church of the Nazarene with a friend. Her dad was the new preacher with a daughter my age. I became friends with her and began attending their church. After high school graduation I went to Bethany Nazarene College (now Southern

Nazarene University) with Martha and other friends from church. College had never really entered my thoughts and plans but they thought I should go with them. Because I got my eyes on people and events around me, I slipped in my Christian experience and became very disillusioned. When I went home for the summer, I was very bitter and wanted nothing more to do with the church. It was only after I was married and had a child that I started attending church again. Even then I only had a surface type Christianity. It was only after my husband died and the Lord sent me to Nazarene Bible College in Colorado Springs that I dedicated my life to Christ and became more rooted in Him. My Christian walk has been a rocky experience but now I am grounded in Him.

Gardening And Good Eating

A big garden was almost always a necessity in our lives. We had to supplement the groceries we bought to make then stretch enough to feed all of us. Each boss usually had a milk cow and we shared the milk since Daddy did the milking. (Something I never learned to do was milk a cow.) I can remember running up the road to meet Daddy as he carried those milk pails home. I loved to drink the warm milk, even before it had been run through the separator. We didn't mind running the separator but we sure didn't like cleaning it up afterward. That was a hard job, taking it all apart, washing each piece thoroughly and then putting it all back together, but it had to be done to keep the milk clean and sterile. We would pour the milk into gallon jars and let the cream rise to the top so it could be skimmed off to make butter or sell in town at the local creamery. The cream would then be churned into butter, either with a paddle churn or simply be shaking it in a jar if the churn was broken. We also had a few eggs to sell from time to time. We would make our own cottage cheese by setting a pan of milk on the warm wood stove until it clabbered. Seasonings were added to taste. We thought it tasted good back then but might not today since we've grown accustomed to the commercial version.

Our garden vegetables consisted of the basics: tomatoes, green beans, peas, corn, radishes, onions, cucumbers, watermelons, pumpkins and cantaloupe. Sometimes we might try carrots, lettuce and okra or others. One year we planted some popcorn just to see if it would produce. We had a good crop and ate lots of popcorn that year. Our largest garden, and the one I remember most, was at the May Valley house. We lived on a large corner, probably once part of the field, plus we got to use part of another field. We kids were all old enough by then to be a big help tending it. When the vegetables were ripe, we ate well and also did a lot of canning so we could also eat well during the winter. Canning days were hot days spent in the kitchen with the wood stove kept hot and no air conditioning. We didn't particularly enjoy all that hot work but we knew it had to be done if we wanted to eat.

In the dry southeastern corner of Colorado, rainfall was not always plentiful. We had no well to draw from and we couldn't use our drinking water from the cistern because the boss paid for that. If there was irrigation water in the adjoining field, we could divert some of it to flood and water the garden, but those times were few and far between. (The boys caught a large catfish in the irrigation ditch once and Mama fried it up for us to eat.) We had to have other ways to water our garden so it would produce well. We lived about a mile from a lake and the runoff water went into a sort of creek we called the seep ditch. It was located about a quarter of a mile from our house and served different purposed for us. It was the main source of water for our garden but it meant we had to carry our water buckets that far during the hot days of summer. The good part was that the seep ditch wasn't very deep and had a nice rocky bottom. We spent many hours without our shoes and socks frolicking in that cool water. Many years we had fresh vegetables to exhibit at the county fair if we could get Daddy or some neighbor to help us get them there. We did win our fair share of ribbons on them.

Since our family was large, it took quite a lot to feed all of us. The garden certainly helped. We spent quite a bit of time cutting up and deseeding pumpkins when they were ripe. We loved pumpkin pie but we hardly ever got it as such. Instead, we just mixed the filling and baked it in a large roaster pan. It didn't make sense to spend all that time and trouble mixing and rolling out pie crust when we liked the filling best anyway. We saved making crust for other kinds of pies. When Mama did make pie crust, she would bake the leftover pieces sprinkled with cinnamon and sugar for us to snack on. The boss usually had a beef or two butchered each year and we shared the meat. His family wasn't fond of the organ meats so we got them. I remember eating liver, heart, tongue, brains and even some other internal organs. It made

Chicken Bristles

for a diverse menu. He occasionally had a hog butchered and we had lots of pork. Sometimes we would fry our own pork rinds to snack on. Once we ended up canning some of the pork as we had no freezer. We did have an icebox for some of the years but the ice had to be brought from town and we couldn't always afford it. We did finally get a used refrigerator but it wasn't always reliable. We raised chickens and sometimes a pig or two. We butchered the occasional chicken for eating and had plenty of eggs to eat, fixed many different ways. The pigs were usually sent to market and sold to help buy school clothes and supplies. We colored lots of hard-boiled eggs at Easter and spent hours hiding and hunting them. Each child got a turn at hiding so it took quite a while for everyone to get a turn. The eggs were usually not in very good condition when we finally finished our playing with them but they were still eaten.

Pinto beans were not something we grew. However, they were cheap and we ate lots of beans and cornbread. Daddy once brought home a large burlap bag of beans straight from the harvest field. They had to be carefully cleaned before we could cook them as they still had all the debris from the field in them. I think this was during one of our harder times so we ate lots of beans and cornbread for a while. They were good and filling and we were thankful to have them. I remember watching my dad once pour syrup on his beans. I liked beans and I liked syrup so thought surely they would be good, especially if my daddy ate them that way. UGH! I think it was some of the worst stuff I had ever tasted. I still like beans but I certainly don't put syrup on them.

The boss hunted birds some and one year shot a goose. His wife didn't want to mess with it, so he gave it to us. That bird was really hard to scald and pluck. We did finally get it cleaned and cooked after a lot of hard work. Mama said, "I don't care if he ever brings us another goose. He can just clean it himself." She didn't appreciate all the hard work for such a small meal. We made chocolate cake a lot, naturally from scratch. No sense splurging on mixes (if they even had them back then) when we had all the ingredients available for less. We used the recipe on the back of the Hershey's cocoa can. It made a large cake; it was good and also easy to make. There was always a lot of fussing and arguing about who would get to lick the spoon and bowl. One time after Mama had mixed up a cake, she just set it down in front of us and told us to "have at it." We ate almost all of that cake batter before we got full up of it. I don't think she had enough left to bake, so we probably had to finish it all. I still prefer just the raw batter instead of baked cake. We didn't always have powdered sugar so our cakes very seldom got frosted. We didn't care. We just loved cake any way we could get it.

Babysitting

Since I wasn't fully responsible for the younger children, I didn't get a lot of actual babysitting experience. Mama didn't work outside the home and seldom went anywhere without us. I did have to help supervise and help with their care, so I did get some experience. My first actual babysitting job was working for a neighbor who had a mentally and physically handicapped child. He couldn't do anything except lie in his carrier. All I had to do was stay with him and keep him clean and fed. I think that was the summer after I graduated from eighth grade. They got him admitted to an institution so the job didn't last long but I did get a little experience.

It's been so long ago that I don't remember exactly how I got acquainted with Betty and Harry, but we had a long working and friendly relationship.

Babysitting

Betty and Harry: I started as the babysitter and
ended as friends. I considered them my second family.

They needed someone to stay with their three children while Betty worked on Saturdays and Harry was out working the farm. The kids were all in school during the week. They lived several miles from us but I had the convenience of riding the school bus further along the route and then walking just a mile to their house. I stayed with them on Friday night so I was there when Betty went to work early Saturday morning. I would fix the Saturday noon meal and do some cleaning and laundry. Many times, I would also stay Saturday night as it might be late when Betty got home and they wouldn't have to take the extra time to take me home. Many times, I would attend church with them on Sundays before they took me home. We became good friends over the years. Since the kids weren't real young, they were easy to care for and we had lots of fun. Harry got them to call me "Ellen Baker, the candlestick maker." It stuck.

Several things about being their babysitter stand out in my mind more than others. One Saturday morning Betty had put a chicken on to cook before she went to work. She told me that after it had cooked for a certain length of time to take it out of that pan, put it in another pan and put it in the oven to brown for lunch. After it had cooked the specified time, I turned off the fire and went about doing something else. Soon I went back to the kitchen and opened the pan. POW! The lid flew off that pan and the chicken flew out and up. I had chicken parts and juices clear to the ceiling, down the wall, on the stove and on the floor. OH MY! What do I do now? I sure didn't want Betty or Harry to find out what I had done. My cooler side kicked in. I picked up all the chicken as best I could, put it in the pan and into the oven to brown. I spent a lot of time cleaning up all that mess before Harry and the kids came in for lunch.

They ate the chicken and no one was the wiser about what had happened. I had certainly not been familiar with those newer, small pot-sized pressure cookers and didn't realize what it was until it exploded. I just thought it was a saucepan. We had a huge pressure cooker at home but Mama was the one who took control of it and made sure the pressure was down before it was opened. I never wanted another pressure cooker after that. I don't even want one of the InstaPots so popular today.

When Betty came home that evening, I had no intention of confessing my accident. To begin with, she was not in a good mood at all. As she was relating her bad day, check bouncing, bad day at work, etc., I thought to myself, "There's no way I'm going to add to that." However, as supper and the evening progressed, I just could not keep her in the dark about it. I related it all. She burst out laughing and laughed so hard she cried. As she was wiping the tears from her eyes she said, "I really needed something like that after the day I've had." Harry laughed and declared it was the best chicken he had ever eaten. It's something to look back on and laugh at now but I sure wasn't laughing that day.

Harry was quite a cut-up and always joking about something. He was a short man and had a pot belly. One weekend when I was staying with them, we were both up and about early. Betty was in the bathroom getting ready for the day and Harry only had his jeans on, no shirt. He poked that belly out, rubbed it and casually asked, "What do you think, Baker? A boy or a girl?" I was a naïve teenager but had grown up with two older brothers so I was used to joking and kidding. I shot right back at him, "As big as it is, it will probably be an elephant." He hooted out a big laugh, slapped his leg and said, "That's what my wife thinks, too. She said she's already felt its trunk." I was so embarrassed and must have turned bright red. He just laughed and Betty did, too, when he told her, even though she got onto him for embarrassing me that way. He laughed about that for years.

Harry was a kidder and lots of fun but sometimes just plain ornery. They had a nephew who was somewhat of a picky eater at times and Harry didn't help matters any. The family was trying to get this young boy to eat cottage cheese. They went through all the arguments and reasons why he should at least taste it and finally had him convinced. Just as he was about to try it, Harry stuck out his tongue and went, "Bleah" and made a terrible face. No tasting for the boy. After a long time and much effort, they had again convinced him to take a bite. Harry was admonished to stay quiet so as not to discourage the child. He sat quietly. Just as the boy was about to get the spoon to his mouth, Harry went, "Bleah," again with that terrible face. That was it. The child was done with cottage cheese forever. For as long as I knew them, I don't think that boy ever did eat cottage cheese. Harry always thought it was funny and repeatedly told the story. The family gave him a good talking to, but it didn't really faze him. He still thought it was funny.

We stayed close friends for years, even after I married and had kids of my own. A trip home to visit my parents also meant a visit to Betty and Harry until they moved away. Once when I went to visit, it had been quite a while since I had been to see them so we had lots of catching up to do. We sat at the kitchen table and visited for a long time. Finally, I got up and headed for the door to leave. Harry said, "Sit down and stay awhile, Baker. It's been a long time since we've seen you." So, I sat down and the visiting continued. This happened several times. Finally, Harry got up and said, "Baker, you can stay and visit with Betty if you want to, but I'm going to bed." Betty just laughed. She said to me, "You were the one who kept trying to leave and he kept urging you to stay." I did finally take my leave and go back to my parents' house but it was another thing we laughed about through the years. Friends like that don't come along very often. I mourned along with them when they lost a teenage son in a tragic accident and a granddaughter in another. Betty and Harry are both dead now. I still miss them and keep their memories alive.

4-H

Growing up in a rural community almost guaranteed that 4-H would become part of our lives. Just in case you are not familiar with it, the 4 Hs stand for Head, Hands, Health and Heart. I think we could join at nine years old. I'm not sure if Maureen was ever in 4-H but the rest of us were. She was somewhat of a rebel and had her own ideas. Because she was the oldest, she could sometimes get away with things the rest of us couldn't. 4-H gave us a chance to get together with other kids in the community in the summer and also get involved in activities we ordinarily wouldn't have been able to. It was a great learning experience. There were so many different projects from which to choose: cooking, sewing, animals, arts and crafts, leadership and others. We always had different animals to raise and the garden vegetables so we had projects. I was always involved in the cooking and sewing as well as animals. The boys stuck more to gardening and animals. I learned different skills

4-H

in 4-H and got to travel to places I wouldn't have been able to otherwise. My involvement included judging, plays, skits and square dancing. There were local competitions in most of these activities as well as state and national. I was lucky enough to go to state in several different categories at different times. These were usually held on the campus of Colorado State University in Fort Collins and we got to stay in the dorms. I loved those trips that were held over a period of several days.

I started my 4-H career in sewing, making a simple scarf and apron. I kept that scarf well into my married life even though I didn't use it. It was just packed away in a box with other mementos. I progressed up the ladder until I was making different types of dresses. Too bad I didn't keep up with that knowledge and ability. I don't sew at all these days; can barely sew on a button. My cooking skills went from simple cookies to fancy breads. A friend and I once did a team demonstration on how to make Easter egg braided bread. When the judge asked the question, "Why do you not add more flour after the bread rises?", I looked at Betty to see if she wanted to answer it. She was looking bewildered so I answered the question correctly, "You don't add more flour after the bread rises because it will leave streaks in the dough." She told me later, "I sure was glad you answered that question because I had no idea what the answer was." That was one of the good parts of doing a team demonstration: you got to share the work and both got credit even if both didn't know all the answers. I did a single demonstration once making chocolate no bake cookies. We made them at home quite often so I was fairly proficient at making them. The problem began when I arrived at the demonstration room. The stove I was to use was electric and all we had at home was a wood stove. That was something I had not even considered. I don't think I had even seen an electric stove before that. I managed to pull it off but I sure had to think of a lot of patter to fill in the time while the stove was even heating. As I stated earlier, I had lots of learning experiences.

One of the requirements within a project I had chosen one year was to plan, cook, execute and document a party of some type. We were not a party-giving family. So, what was I to plan and carry out? I was probably thirteen or so that year and really knew nothing about giving a party. I had attended a birthday party or two so I decided on a birthday party. I settled om a party for my youngest sister, Sherry. Since her birthday was at the end of January, nasty cold weather season, I decided to hold the party in the summer when the weather was nicer and the guests might be able to play outside. I don't think any of us had ever had a birthday party with invited guests. She would be the first. Because my birthday is in June, I settled on that date even though the party would be for Sherry. The weather cooperated; it was a beautiful day for everyone to be outdoors. I had to plan the whole affair, games to play as well as bake the cake.

4-H

It was my birthday, but in her honor, so she got the gifts. When her friends learned that it was actually my birthday, they ganged up and gave me the birthday spanking. That just did not seem to be fair, somehow. It did turn out quite nicely and I got credit for my work. I doubt if Sherry ever got another birthday party as a child.

4-H led me in many directions and gave me many opportunities I otherwise wouldn't have experienced. Since Mama didn't drive, I had to rely on neighbors and/or 4-H leaders to get me where I needed to be. Many times, we met at a leader's house or maybe at the school house, depending on the project we were working on. I enjoyed going to a leader's house because they were always so much nicer than mine. They also had electric sewing machines whereas ours was an old treadle that I didn't like to use much. But I did. We always had to show off what we had done, either at the county fair or the 4-H revues. We always had a dress revue for our sewing projects that we had to model for the public.

Modeling my dress at one of the annual 4-H dress revues.

Those were usually held at the Lamar Community Building which was used for almost every type of event from sports to floor shows. It had a high stage with dressing rooms beneath, meeting rooms on various levels and bleachers. It was a very popular and well used venue. One year before I started high school, we were there practicing for our dress revue which would be held that evening. I don't remember what I was doing on the stage. But I do

4-H

remember starting to walk around the curtain which was open at the time. The next thing I remember, I was lying at the top of the stairs which led down to the dressing rooms beneath. People were hovering over me, asking if I was all right. That fall was probably ten or twelve feet easily. They took me to a doctor to be checked over but I was fine, only had a small cut on one ear. The doctor explained that I was still young enough that my bones were still soft enough that nothing broke. If I had been older, I might have been seriously injured. The show went on as scheduled and I modeled whatever I had made that year.

Animals were a big part of our lives so that naturally carried over into 4-H. We never had expensive, high-quality animals as so many do today. Our hogs were just ordinary, run-of-the-mill animals. Our sheep were usually the orphan lambs from the boss' flock as he didn't like to bottle feed them. The biggest problem we had with the sheep was that Daddy didn't get around to bobbing their tails as early as it should have been done. He was always too busy working for the boss to do things for us that needed to be done. He was experienced at bobbing tails and didn't want us doing it. We just continued doing what had to be done with what we had. We almost always had an animal to show at the fair each year even if it was a scrub.

Chicken Bristles

Me with one of many 4-H sheep. Daddy hadn't gotten this ones' tail bobbed yet.

I think I stayed in 4-H longer than my older brothers as they got involved in sports once they entered high school. Then they got jobs helping other farmers in the summers. Roger was going to raise quail for a special project one summer. He housed them in a former hog house quite a distance from our house so they would be in a quiet place. One night we heard quite a commotion coming from that direction. When we went to investigate, we found an opossum had invaded the house and was killing all the baby quail.

4-H

Roger managed to hit it hard with a shovel and it went limp. He was sure he had killed it. He carried it to the house and threw it down, intending to bury it later. When he went out to bury it, that opossum had indeed been 'playing 'possum' and run off once there was no one around. Another lesson learned: make sure the dead opossum is really dead.

My friend Betty's father (different Betty than the babysitting chapter) was the local county agent. He got her involved in a program raising Landrace hogs which had been donated to introduce the breed. Whoever was awarded a female had to then donate a female piglet to someone else the next year. I was lucky enough to be awarded one of those beautiful, long white hogs to raise.

Me with my beautiful Landrace sow.

Chicken Bristles

I sure was proud of her. I took very good care of her and showed her at the county fair. I don't remember winning any ribbons with her but I was certainly proud to show her off. I usually had to show those scrubby sheep, so this, too, was another new experience in showmanship. I even bought a pair of cowboy boots (my first) to wear while showing her. I don't remember who got one of the piglets from her litter or even what happened to her or any of the other piglets she had.

No matter what our projects were, we had to keep records of what we had done and turn them in at the end of the year. I think those records books were even judged to see who had kept the best records. I wasn't too great with the individual records but I did get a trophy one year for keeping the best club records and scrapbook. I kept that trophy for a long time, finally donating it to some charitable organization to be reused.

Our county wide 4-H awards banquet was held in the fall after all activities were concluded for the year. It was held in the community building and was a bring-a-dish meal. There were always table after table of delicious food. We always tried to attend this event; even my mother usually attended with us. Not only did one or more of us most likely get some type of award or recognition, we knew there would be lots of good food to eat, some we didn't even know what it was. With so much good food and

4-H

different varieties, my mother always managed to overeat. I can remember many times she would go home from this event so miserable from her overindulgence that she would go out into the back yard and make herself throw up just to get some relief. She sure enjoyed the eating part though because there were so many foods she didn't get to indulge in at home. I can't remember everything we ever took, but I do seem to remember a cranberry salad we used to make. We loved it and I guess others did too because I don't think we ever got to take much of it home. How we loved those banquets! Lots of good food is a luxury for poor people.

My 4-H career probably ended the summer before I became a Junior in high school. I wanted to work to help pay my expenses and have some spending money. Since Mama didn't drive and Daddy usually worked late and couldn't always be relied on to ferry me back and forth to town, my folks decided that if I could find a family to stay with, I could move to town for work and school. I lived with a young couple that first year and went to work at the A&W drive-in. Living with that family didn't pan out for long but I found another family and lived with them for the rest of my high school years. I worked at the A&W for two or three summers. I still had to walk several miles to work from school but one of my co-workers would take me home so I wouldn't have to walk that far late at night. I loved that job and all the wonderful people I met there.

County Fair

The culmination for the year of 4-H and summer was the county fair. It was held in August, coinciding with the Lamar Days celebration. I'm not sure if there was always a parade but I do remember one year our 4-H club had a float in the parade. Our motto was "As the twig is bent, so grows the tree." I think I do remember working on other floats over the years but this is the only one that stands out in my mind.

County Fair

One of our 4-H floats with the theme,
'As the twig is bent, so grows the tree'.

The weather was hot and dry at this time of year. Maybe we did have an occasional rain but it wasn't usually a problem. One year I do remember was a little different though. The fairgrounds were way south of Lamar's town proper. I had gone downtown for some reason and there came one of those unexpected summer rain showers; I got caught in it. When I got back to the fairgrounds, not a drop of rain had fallen there. I had a hard time convincing some of them that it had actually rained. The rain has to stop somewhere and it stopped before it reached the fairgrounds that time. Many years later I was standing on one side of a dry street and watching it rain on the other side of it. It looks a little strange.

Even with the weather being so hot, we always enjoyed the county fair. It was exciting to see all the wonderful exhibits, including our own, plus all the other activities going on. There was a carnival with all those daredevil rides and, of course, the sideshows and games of chance on the midway. Because we had 4-H projects to display and animals to show, we usually got to spend all day there, usually more than one. Many times, we had to catch a ride with neighbors as Daddy was too busy working to take us. Our 4-H leaders made sure we got there as we had to enter or display our projects. Some projects were still to be judged, such as showing all the animals. We had to parade them in the show ring before judges and spectators. I don't remember ever winning any ribbons for my animals or showmanship but it was great fun and a learning experience. Each club also had a booth to showcase some of what the members had accomplished over the summer. Some of the best sewing and food products were on display in it. Even the booths were judged for how well they were presented.

The 4-H activities were pretty well over by this time of year. The dress revue had been held earlier in the summer. Our demonstrations had been performed and judged, the livestock and crop judging were over and we had to have our record books completed except for what we were doing at

County Fair

the fair. Some of the winning exhibits would go on to the state fair which was in the latter part of August or early September. I don't remember what all the circumstances were or why I got to go, but I do remember spending several days or a week for 4-H at the state fair one summer. I even acquired a boyfriend while there. I was very embarrassed when some of my friends and fellow campers wrote a poem about it and had it read in front of everyone at one of our meals. It was doubly worse because I was so shy back then and hated being singled out in public. I kept a copy of that poem for a long time before it finally got lost in a move. It was titled "A State Fair Love Affair" and one of the lines said something about wearing 'more lipstick and straight hair.' That was also the year I got burned out on carnival rides. My boyfriend and I were wandering around the carnival grounds one afternoon before the carnival was open. The operators were checking the Ferris wheel to make sure everything was working right and offered us a ride. Of course, we were eager for a free ride to help with their testing. That ride going round and round seemed to go on forever. I finally had to have them stop it so I could get off as I thought I was going to be sick. After standing on solid ground for a while my stomach settled down and I was fine. That was pretty much the end of my carnival riding days. I do remember one more experience with rides when I was in college. There were two amusements parks in Oklahoma City at that time. My date and I started talking about which roller coaster was better. Since I had never ridden on one, he offered to give me the thrill. We went to one park and then the other just to ride the roller coaster. I don't remember much about either one so I must not have been too impressed or else I was so scared I just blocked it from my mind. I don't really remember riding much after that and especially not a Ferris wheel!

The county fair was not just for 4-H project displays and judging. There were just as many or more open classes for anyone who wanted to enter something. Since we had to be there anyway, my mother took advantage and entered different classes, usually baked and/or canned goods. She usually won some ribbons even though they weren't grand champions. If something was good enough for a ribbon it had a small amount of money attached to it which she received from her fair entries each year. One canning entry that she won a ribbon on several times was her watermelon pickles. Since we grew so many watermelons, we had lots of rinds to peel and cook. We didn't mind this too much as we sure enjoyed the eating of those pickles. There were not a lot of entries in that class because many people didn't even know what they were.

Mama baked cakes and cookies often but those took extra flour and sugar that we could not always afford. We canned every year just to keep food on the table, so why not show some of it off? One year she had found a new lemon pie recipe that she wanted to try. It was going to be a little more expensive to make so she saved it for the fair. I seem to recall that it was called something like a lemon cake pie. Naturally since it was going to be more experience to make, she could only make one. That meant we did not get to sample it before it went to be judged at the fair. When we checked on it after the judging was over, it had won a ribbon (blue for first if I remember correctly). WOW! Now we really couldn't wait to get it home so we could at least have a small sample of it. We had to wait until it was released a day or so later until we could do anything about it. Naturally it had to be one of those times that we had to wait on Daddy to get us there, so we were late picking everything up. The first place we headed was to the building where the baked goods were. When we arrived there all we found was the pie plate with the ribbon draped across it and a few crumbs. Someone else must have thought it looked good too and maybe we weren't coming back for it. We were sure mad about it and very disappointed but there was nothing we could do about it except take our empty plate, go home and see if we could talk Mama into making another one for us. Ironically, she couldn't remember where she had found that recipe. We never did get to taste that pie. Even to this day I still wonder what it would taste like or what it was even called. I know it was not just a run-of-the-mill pie. Lemon is still my favorite pie today.

Chicken Bristles

One year in conjunction with the fair and Lamar Days celebration, a beard growing contest was announced. I don't remember Daddy ever having whiskers. He would faithfully wash and shave every day. He even used a shaving mug with the brush and suds instead of getting his shaving cream from a can. Many times, he even used a straight razor, stropping it to get it really sharp. That one year he decided to grow a beard. It did make him look more distinguished. He didn't win any prize and was very eager to get it shaved off. It was so coarse and stiff that he had trouble shaving it. Mama had to get the scissors and snip a lot of it off before he could actually shave. When he finally did get it off, he swore it was the last time he would ever let his whiskers grow that long. He never did again. He might have skipped shaving for a day or so now and then but that was the extent of it. We liked his smooth leathery cheeks.

This And *That*

When my mind goes wandering back over the years, there are so many memories that float through it. It's impossible to recall everything we did as children and it's easier to remember the good times. I know we had problems and troubles. No life is perfect even when we try to pretend it is. I cherish all the experiences that made me what I am today even though I didn't think I would back then. Many memories are fleeting but worth recalling.

Even though there were many of us, we did all get along fairly well. Maureen left home at an early age so she doesn't enter into a lot of memories. I do remember going to her house in Syracuse, Kansas, after she was married. She fed us fried rabbit which I had never eaten before. We didn't see her a lot after she got married at an early age. I did live in town with her one summer after her divorce and took care of her two children while she worked.

Chicken Bristles

Except for the few normal childhood diseases, we were all pretty healthy, considering. We lived in a drafty, old house, cold in winter and hot in summer. We played in the dirt, ran around barefoot most of the summer and sometimes even in the winter. Our clothes were probably not always adequate for the weather and we didn't have vitamins and such to supplement our, many times, inadequate diet. Mentholatum, Vick's salve and cod liver oil were our remedies for colds and stuffy noses. Mama would sometimes make a mustard compress for a chest cold. Except for that fall from the stage (4-H chapter), I don't remember visiting a doctor or dentist until much later in life. Our polio and smallpox vaccinations were given at school. Several times I had some kind of red, itchy bumps on my hands but never knew what caused them. I used to rub them with bleach trying to relieve that itch. Once I got past childhood, I've never had any more occurrences of them. I had a bump on my wrist that my brothers would push on, trying to get it to shrink. I learned later that this was probably called a ganglion. It disappeared without my even being aware of it and has never reappeared. Good health has been with me well into my later years.

My two older brothers got along with each other very well. Most of the time they were best friends. I can also recall some fights and chases around the house with the threat, "I'll kill you if I catch you." The next time I saw them they would have their arms around each other and were best friends again. I was closer in age to them than my younger sister so I was a big tomboy and played more with them. They had their mean times too, though. I don't remember what happened but I remember trying to hit Roger in the head with the hammer while he slept. Thankfully someone stopped me and took the hammer away from me before I could do him any damage.

My father didn't have any teeth. I think he had them all pulled when I was quite young. He couldn't afford dentures so he was just toothless. As time passed, his gums became very tough and he could eat almost anything, even steak. The only thing I can recall him not eating was corn on the cob. Mama always cut it off for him. His gums were so tough that he could draw blood on our fingers If he bit us hard enough. We didn't test that very often because we knew he could do it. He functioned quite well with no teeth and never seemed to be self-conscious about it.

The May Valley house was old and not sealed very well so the wind blew in through all the cracks. All of us kids slept upstairs which consisted of two huge rooms. Many times in the winter when it snowed and the wind was blowing, we would wake to a dusting of snow on our beds. We didn't notice the dust quite as much in the summer but it came in just the same. At least once we had a really bad dust storm. I remember Mama hanging blankets and sheets over doors and windows as well as stuffing cracks trying to keep the dust out as much as possible. It did help but lots of dust and dirt still filtered through. It probably wasn't as bad as the huge dust storms of the thirties but it was still bad enough.

We had trees along two sides of the property, many of which were mulberry. We would often put old sheets on the ground to catch the mulberries as we shook the trees. More often we would just pick the berries directly from the tree and eat them. Thet were good but messy. We had purple fingers a lot during the summer. The birds loved them too and they could really make a purple mess wherever they pooped, especially on vehicles or clothes hanging on the line.

We only had a wringer washer and no dryer so everything was hung outside on long clotheslines. We also had to draw the water from the cistern and heat it on the wood stove. Wash day was always an all-day long project. The clothes always smelled nice and fresh from hanging on the line in the fresh air. It was miserable hanging them out in the winter. Sometimes we would let them freeze dry and other times we ended up taking them in early and hanging them indoors anywhere we could find to hang them; draped over chairs, on hooks or even lines we had stretched across rooms. Winter was not always pretty at our house.

An apricot tree grew just to one side of the house. It didn't bear a lot of fruit but there was enough for me to climb up into that tree and eat apricots. I loved them even though I don't think the others liked them that well. I actually burned out on them and didn't eat them again for many years.

Me posing in front of our apricot tree. Part of the rear portion of our house is in the background.

There was a huge pear tree in our yard that had become intertwined with a locust or some other type of prickly tree. It grew large pears at the very top but we couldn't climb the tree to pick them. We did get a few when they ripened enough to fall to the ground. The pears on the bottom branches were small, hard and bitter. We tried cooking them a few times but it didn't help much. Daddy had put up a swing on one of the lower branches in that tree. That spot pretty much became my private retreat. I spent many, many hours out there just daydreaming and thinking. I planned a lot of futures under that tree.

The boss usually had a herd of sheep in the winter which he kept in a feedlot. We liked to go with Daddy in the evening to feed them. For several years there were a couple of filled silage pits used for feed. We liked to ride down into them when Daddy filled the pickup bed with that stinky silage. One winter the boss rented a large pasture for the herd. He hired a sheepherder to stay out there with them night and day. This man had his small sheepherder's trailer and it had everything in it he needed. Those were tiny houses before the tiny houses of today became popular. We loved to go watch him work with his dog and the sheep. The sheep would be let out into a larger pasture during the day and gathered into a smaller space at night. It was amazing how the two of them (man and dog) would work together to get the sheep where they should be.

When I was very young Daddy would buy a few fireworks for the 4th of July. He did most of the lighting of larger items and we were allowed some sparklers to twirl around. As we got older, I don't remember having fireworks very often. When we lived at May Valley the boss's retired father would, for many years, treat us with a case of soda pop for the 4th. We didn't get soda pop very often so that was really a treat for us.

We used to visit one of Daddy's sisters, Willa Belle, quite often on Sunday afternoons. As I got older and spent more time away from home, I didn't get to visit her very often. Once when I was back home, I went to visit her. I made the comment, "I don't think I've seen you in about five years." She said, "Well, five years isn't such a long time." It sounded like forever to me. Now that I am older, I realize how right she was. Five years isn't such a long time after all.

When we are young, time seems to pass very slowly. As we age it seems to pick up speed and move along much faster. These memories seem to have happened such a long time ago and yet some of them are very fresh in my mind. I'm sure there are many more stuck further back and only get remembered when something triggers them. Memories can be such wonderful things. They not only remind us of the past but also helped shape us into the people we are today. There are good ones, bad ones, sad ones and happy ones. Some we like to remember more than others but we cannot change any of them. They will always be a part of us. Carry yours with you; take them out and examine them from time to time. Give thanks to God that he has given you the time to reflect on them. Your memories are you. Treasure them all.

About The Author

EJ has lived in several states in the central United States due to marriage, college and moving closer to family. This book takes a very different turn from her first writing experience and published work, 'Life Lessons from Solitaire'. She experienced a variety of childhood exploits and adventures and has also had a diverse work history, having experiences in the food industry, oil and gas, insurance and banking fields as well as volunteering at a local hospital. She has been widowed for many years and has a son and daughter. She currently lives in Oklahoma with her daughter and two cats.

www.ingramcontent.com/pod-product-compliance
Lightning Source LLC
LaVergne TN
LVHW020448070526
838199LV00063B/4882